Small Space Gardening for Busy People

Grow Food with Limited Space and Time

Urbanehaus.com
antoine@urbanehaus.com

A N D R E   K I N G

Table of Contents

INTRODUCTION

Gardening can be a nice hobby a lifelong passion or something you have always loathed. Whether you are a hobby gardener, seriously passionate about it or you loath gardening and hate getting your hands dirty I hope you will take the time to read through this book and use it as a guide towards a healthier and more fulfilling life. I'm assuming you do not loath gardening as you most probably would not have bought this book if that were the case. So, I'm hoping you have a basic interest and an eagerness to learn.

In this book I focus on how to use the space you have got to your advantage. You don't need a huge front yard or a backyard to start a garden. You can pretty much start a garden anywhere you want to. What you do need to have is a good imagination and a willingness to try out new things.

You can use containers such as flower and plant pots to create a productive garden! Small space gardening will enable you to utilize small spaces to create a beautiful garden. I'm all about utility so if you are just interested in decorative flowers this may not be the book for you. I like to grow things that I can use in the kitchen and which save me money and a trip to the grocery store.

The ideas in this book focus mainly on outdoor small space gardening. If you have no outdoor space whatsoever then check out another book of mine The indoor Herb gardeners' companion as this details how to start a herb garden indoors.

Let me paint a picture for you. It's late afternoon on a sunny September Sunday. The sky is deep blue the trees glow golden in the sunlight. Wherever you are in the world wouldn't you love to be out in the garden harvesting your early Fall crop? The idea of enjoying homegrown produce does sound enticing, doesn't it? With the help of this book, you will be able to enjoy all this and much more.

In this book, you will learn about small space gardening, find different ideas to create a garden, find a selection of ideal plants to grow and tips and steps to start the garden, including details of the necessary tools and much more. Once you are through with this book, you will be able to start your small space garden in a heartbeat.

CHAPTER ONE:

Benefits of Gardening

"I grow plants for many reasons: to please my eye or to please my soul, to challenge the elements or to challenge my patience, for novelty or for nostalgia, but mostly for the joy in seeing them grow." – David Hobson

Everyone has their own reasons, motivations and drive for gardening. Is the case for life itself. Essentially everyone needs a passion to give life to their years. Without passion life tends to be rather dull and lackluster. Most passions started out as interests or hobbies before they bloomed into fully fledged passions. Most of us work with either people or machines. If your work day consists of emails, computers phone calls and meetings gardening is a great contrast and will feel like a breath of fresh air. It is a brilliant way to unwind after a hectic day. There are a multitude of benefits to gardening and, in this section, you will learn specifically about the advantages of small space gardening.

Better-tasting produce

Homegrown produce, regardless of whether it is fruit, vegetables or even herbs, tastes much better than what you can buy at your local supermarket. Organically grown produce is richer in nutrients and minerals when compared to commercially grown food.

Cost-effective

An obvious benefit of gardening is that you can save money when you grow your produce at home. For instance, if you have a mixed planter of different herbs, you will always have fresh herbs readily available. Not only are the herbs fresher, they are cheaper as well. You need a packet of seeds to plant the plants and that's the initial cost of harvest. You will effectively spend only a fraction of what you usually do. You can even dry the harvest and preserve them.

Relaxing

If you want a hobby that will relax you, then gardening is a good idea. The joy of watching your garden grow and thrive is a pleasure like no other. With small space gardening, you don't have to worry about any space restrictions as well. A little creativity and you can pretty much turn anything into a micro-garden. It is very gratifying to cook with your own home grown produce. Gardening is therapeutic in that the physical tasks require focus and concentration which enables you to let go of stress and anxiety. In this sense it can also be meditative.

Conscious eating and nutrition

Gardening will teach you a thing or two about conscious eating. Most of us don't give a thought to the food that we eat or the ingredients that we cook with. When you nurture a plant and watch it grow, you will appreciate how valuable it is. It makes you more aware of what goes into and what it takes to create vegetables. You will finally be able to appreciate not just the produce on your table, but the efforts of all those who make the produce available to you.

Knowledge is power

Learning by doing! You will learn about the process of gardening when you start to cultivate food in your garden. The best way to learn is to do. Since you are the one that will prepare the soil, plant, nurture, fertilize and water the plants the learning curve is steady but constant. Store-bought produce will never teach you anything about the manner in which it is all grown.

Design element

Plants are all the rage. Just flick through a home design or architecture magazine and you will see a plant is most room mock ups. Adding a plant or two to your home will certainly brighten up your living space. A small garden will enhance your homes appearance. A dash of green, a speck of blue and a hint lavender will brighten up your kitchen and add to your home's appearance.

Seasonal changes

If your garden consists of any seasonal plants, then you might want to switch your garden. However, a small-space garden can be easily made adaptable to any seasonal changes. A small space garden can be made mobile and moved around to make the most of the sun and warmth. If you have your garden in containers on the balcony then it is fairly easy to insulate them in the winter or even bring them inside out of the cold. With a regular garden you will face other seasonal challenges which you don't have to worry about here.

Plant anywhere

One of the many advantages of a small space garden is that it does not necessarily need to be set up outside. You can have your small space garden on the windowsills, balconies, or even have a garden indoors. If there is sufficient sunlight, you can pretty much grow anything you want. Even if you have no outside space at all and insufficient sunlight you can even have an indoor garden with artificial lighting. It might not be the optimal solution but there really are no limitations when it comes to small space gardening. And with no limitations comes no excuses. Regardless of your circumstances you really can plant anywhere. You just need soil, light and water.

CHAPTER TWO:

Key Steps to Start a Small Space Garden

"To plant a garden is to believe in tomorrow" – *Audrey Hepburn*

All gardeners believe in a better future. To start a garden requires a certain amount of patience and the ability to defer gratification. There are a number of steps to take when starting a small space garden which you will learn in this section..

You don't need a huge front yard or a backyard to start a garden. Not only that, you don't need to spend hours on end to start and maintain a garden. Even if you like gardening, you perhaps don't have the time for it given the busy lives people lead. Well, don't you worry - Small space gardening is a brilliant concept that allows you to take part in the joys of gardening even when there is a time and space constraint. The idea is to maximize the harvest and make the best use of space available. To do this, you need to plant the right varieties of plants, prepare the soil and use all the space available- vertical as well as horizontal. That's the gist of it and you will learn more about this simple concept in this book.

Most urban spaces provide the opportunity to take a creative approach toward gardening. There is no such thing as an unsuitable space, as long as you can find a suitable plant to grow. For instance, if you have a lawn, you can add some raised beds to it. You can transform your kitchen window with a raised planter. Perhaps, you can grow a variety of herbs in a big container and add it to your kitchen countertop.

Soil

The first thing that you need to concentrate on for any garden is the soil. The art of small space gardening boils down to three important aspects. The first aspect is to prepare the soil for the plants that you want to grow. The second factor is to select the right variety of plants to grow and the final aspect that you need to consider is the proper utilization of the space available. One aspect of gardening that a lot of people seem to ignore is the soil quality. All soils are usually a mix of sand, clay and silt. Soil contains a mix of organic matter, minerals and different microorganisms. Since you will need to alter the soil or grow the plants in pots, you don't have to worry a lot about the type your garden soil is. That being said, it is a good idea to familiarize yourself with certain soil-related terms. It can be quite overwhelming, especially for a beginner, while going through the different varieties of composts and mixes that are available. One word that you will come across is soilless. What does a soilless mix mean? It simply means a mix that doesn't resemble the usual soil mix that you would find in a regular garden. There are no minerals or microorganism present in a soilless mix.

For a plant, the soil is the natural source of nutrients. Therefore, there is a direct relation between the quality of the soil and the health of the plant. Loamy soil is the best suited for herbs and green vegetables. It is a combination of organic matter, silt and sand. It has sufficient nitrogen, phosphorus and potash, which are necessary for a plant's growth. The pH factor of the soil is essential, and it needs to be within the range of 6 to 7.5. To determine the pH of the soil, you can purchase some pH strips and stick it in the soil. If the pH is less than 6, then you need to add some agricultural lime to the soil. If the pH is higher than 7.3, then you need to add some sulphur. Add organic matter, peat moss or compost to the soil if it is heavy and clayey. The ideal garden soil contains about 25% air and around 25% water.

Select the compost

Any compost that you purchase from a store is a mix of rotted organic matter and a couple of other ingredients like peat or coconut fiber. Compost is a great way to recycle organic matter and dispose of your own garden waste. For more information on making and maintaining a compost heap please visit urbanehaus.com. If you decide to purchase compost then always go for the high-quality variety, even if it might cost a little more. Compost is the source of nutrients that will feed and nourish your garden. It is a good idea to add lime to the soil, except for if you are growing potatoes or any other ericaceous plants. Most of the vegetable plants thrive in an alkaline soil. Add some vermiculture or perlite to the soil. It helps with drainage as well as water retention. You can even add horticultural sand to a couple of tubers like carrots and beets that need less compact soil for their roots to develop.

Feeding

You need to regularly feed and fertilize the plants in your garden if you want healthy plants. Feeding is quite important, and you must not forget about it. When there are space limitations, it is likely that the plants will be planted in close quarters and this can reduce the nutrient content in the soil. All plants need three primary nutrients for their growth and these nutrients are nitrogen (N), phosphorus (P) and potassium (K). Apart from this, they will need other trace minerals in small quantities. You can choose to fertilize the soil once or twice a week according to your convenience. You might wonder why you need to fertilize the soil when you use compost. Well, the minerals and nutrients in the compost last for about 6 weeks and after that, you need to start a regular feeding routine. It is important that you feed the plants and the soil at regular intervals. For any perennial herbs and fruit-bearing plants, you need to remove the top inch or two of the soil and then add some fresh compost before spring or autumn sets in. You need to re-pot the plants once every three years or so. If you think regular feeding is a lot of work, you can always use a slow-release fertilizer that will nourish your plants for about 6 months or so.

Light

Before you start buying any supplies, the first step for starting your own garden is to check whether there is sufficient sunlight or not. It can be your windowsill, area on your patio, or even the rooftop. You can use Google Earth for locating the south-facing area for the sake of planting. A common mistake that most amateur gardeners make is that they end up planting in an area that doesn't receive any sunlight. When selecting the location for your garden it is advisable to track the quality and duration of sunlight it receives. Any kind of plant that produces fruit such as peppers, cucumbers, or even tomatoes will require at least six and a half hours of sunlight per day. With time you will begin to understand the kind of crops that are best suited for the available space. If there isn't sufficient light for a fruiting plant, then in such a case, you can consider growing greens, some herbs and even root vegetables. These plants need at least 4 hours of sunlight every day. If you aren't sure of the amount of sunlight a plant will require, any online catalog will provide you with the required information. If there isn't a well-lit outdoor space available, then in such a case you can consider growing your own herb garden indoors.

Seeds or plants?

Once you have picked a sunny spot, good containers and soil, now is the time to consider whether you want plants or seeds for your garden. Depending on the sunlight available and the accessibility of containers, you can decide what to grow. For a first-time gardener, it is better to start off with starter plants instead of seeds. There are plant varieties for which it is better to start with seeds instead of a plant. Plants like lettuce and various root vegetables don't transplant well, in such a case you start with seeds. If you opt for plants, then the growing season will be short as well. If you chose a summer plant, then in such a case you sow the seeds well before summer so that the saplings can grow. Try starting with plants, and then you can move onto seeds the next time around. Gardening isn't difficult, with the right tools, materials, and patience; you will have a beautiful garden in your home within no time. You will learn about this in the coming chapters.

Garden idea

What is the first thing that comes to your mind when you think about gardening or farming? Probably images of beautiful countryside will pop into your head - Rows of vegetables and orchards of fruit? However, times are changing. An increasing amount of the local food production is slowly shifting to urban areas. This trend is here to stay and it will just increase. This can be done through the small plots of land in the backyard, community gardening, hanging indoor gardens, vertical gardening and even rooftop growing. So, urban gardening is a "thing" now.

Even if you are living in the middle of the urban jungle, you needn't despair. You can still have your own garden. All it takes is a little bit of creativity and you can get started with your very own garden. There are different types of setups that you can make use of for gardening. Use the windowsill, the rooftop, balcony, or even the community garden for growing fresh produce of your own. You will learn more about this in the coming chapters. For more information on this see my other book on the indoor herb gardeners' companion

Pests

Fungus, slugs, whitefly and aphids are the most common pests to trouble the plants in any garden. The two common types of fungus are the blight and the powdery mildew. A simple remedy for the powdery layer of white or grey colored fuzz on the plants is to spray a mixture of milk and water (1:10 ratio) on the affected areas. To treat blight, you simply need to cut off the affected parts. Slugs can be a real pest destroying crops within no time. If you want to go down the chemical route, then buy some organic slug pellets and sprinkle them on the plants. However, it is better to use eco-friendly pest repellents. You can place crushed eggshells or even some gravel around the base of the plant to prevent any pests from crawling onto the plants. Aphids feed on the plant juices and they quite literally suck the life out of the plant. To kill an aphid infestation, mix a mild soap with water and sprinkle this mixture on the plants.

CHAPTER THREE:

Garden Ideas

"You know the best thing about having a house? You get to plant whatever you want in the yard and watch it grow." – Clarissa Pinkola Estes.

Deep containers

You need to choose a container that is at least 14 inches deep if you want to grow vegetables on a rooftop or balcony. If you are growing roots like potatoes, then the container will need to be at least 18 inches deep. With all the containers, you need to monitor the amount of moisture that is present in the soil. Too little or even too much water will impede growth and even cause the roots to rot. While you are growing flowers and vegetables, always make sure that the top 2 inches of the soil is dry before you water it. Overwatering a plant will cause it to rot. Also, be careful while selecting the color of the pot. A dark colored pot tends to absorb more heat than a light colored one. If you are growing succulents, then place the dark-colored pots in the shade during the warmest part of the day. You can repurpose any of the old containers you have at home for the purpose of urban gardening. Make sure that you have cleaned the containers thoroughly before planting. If any chemicals or toxic substances were stored in a container, then it won't be fit for usage. Make use of light potting soil or even a soilless mix. Anything too heavy will lead to poor drainage and even compact the roots. So, don't use garden soil for this purpose.

Window boxes

A window box has access to not just planting, but also weeding, watering and harvesting. It is an effective technique of urban gardening. A window box isn't deep enough to support any deep root plants. You will need to opt for small plants like basil, parsley and various other herbs. Microgreens, leafy vegetables like spinach and lettuce are a really good option that can be considered. Not only does it look fetching, but it also helps in making good use of the space that is available. Just make sure that the window box receives sufficient sunlight before you get started with gardening.

Going vertical

A vertical garden isa container mechanism that will allow you to grow plants in a vertical fashion. Usually, vertical gardens are attached to the wall or they are created in such a manner that they will lean against the wall. Well, it really is that simple and maintaining it is as easy as maintaining a regular garden. If you are just about to start with vertical gardening, then you must learn the basics of selecting a location, the equipment required, types of vertical gardens, selecting the plants and the maintenance of a vertical garden.

For instance, while you are selecting plants, as a gardener you will have to select the ones that will thrive in a vertical garden. Some plants tend to do better than others, like strawberries, any vines or other plants that can be grown well in a container. In the Three Sister's model of gardening, you can grow corn, beans and squash in a single pot. The vines of beans and squash will use the corn stalk for growing. So, you will need to think before you decide on the kind of plants that you will want to grow. Regardless of the plants that you have selected, they will all require sunlight if you want your garden to thrive. So, you will need to select a location where the plants will get ample of sunlight. Gardening vertically can take on many forms. Gardeners can make use of hanging pots, containers placed at different eye levels or even vertical kits.

Green wall

It might have attracted most of the people to vertical gardening. This type of a vertical garden is either free standing or it is attached to the wall, and it can be designed for either indoor or outdoor use. The vegetation or plants that you might want to grow can either encase the entire structure or can be enclosed in a very shallow frame.

Pockets

It is another way of growing plants vertically and in this type of vertical gardening, the containers are made out of breathable felt fabric and resemble pockets in which plants can be grown. You can also make use of a fabric shoe organizer if you are running low on the budget.

Tiered garden

It is essentially made up of long and narrow beds that are arranged in a fashion resembling a staircase. Plants will grow up instead of growing outwards. It might seem more diagonal than vertical, but it still makes a really good use of growing space and will be an ideal fit for urban gardeners who don't have any wall space.

Gutter garden

Yes, you guessed it right. This is a planter that is fashioned out of a normal rain gutter. This can either be arranged in horizontal rows or it can be arranged diagonally so that it facilitates in the better drainage of water. Depending upon the depth of the gutter, the size of the plants that you can grow in it will vary.

Pallet garden

Recycled wood shipping pallets can also be fashioned into a vertical garden. They can be made to lean against a fence or a wall, they can be free standing if they have support posts or even by hanging from the wall. You can make use of them for vertical gardening provided there is some waterproofing material placed between the planter and the structure. For preventing the soil from escaping from the wooden pallets, you can staple landscaping fabric to the sides and the back of the pallet.

Trellis gardens

You might have seen vines that are growing vertically from a trellis, but you might not have realized that you can cover structures of different types and shapes by making use of the vines. You can buy a regular trellis from any of your local gardening supplies store or you can make your own from either wood or wire according to your own requirements. Trellis gardens are perfect for maximizing vertical spaces. Hops, grapes, beans, cucumber, tomatoes, squash are just a few examples of plants that do very well growing vertically.

Vertical garden using PVC pipes

You can design your own garden by making use of PVC pipes by making them stand up straight like a tower or by placing them in horizontal rows against the wall or a fence. In either of the cases, you will simply have to drill holes into your pipes through which your plants can grow. If you are simply letting the pipe stand vertically, then you can plant all around the pipe. Any bushy plant or vine will be ideal and eventually, the plant will cover the entire PVC pipe.

Garden pots

Using garden pots is probably the easiest method to create a vertical garden because you simply have to hang the ceramic or plastic garden pots to the wall. The containers must be arranged closely and in a symmetric manner that will lend a sophisticated look. With multiple individual containers, watering the pots can be easy; plants can also be removed or replaced very easily. Herbs, seasonal, as well as perennial plants, will be best suited for this type of a garden.

Depending on the kind of plants you want to grow and the space that is available, you will have to select a method of gardening. Vertical gardening and container gardening happen to be the two of the most popular methods out there.

CHAPTER FOUR:

Plant Guide

The secret of improved plant breeding, apart from scientific knowledge, is love." – Luther Burbank

Now that you know how to start a small garden, the next step is to select the plants that you want to grow. In this chapter, you will learn about the top ten plants to grow in a small space garden.

Beetroot

Beetroots are very easy to grow and there are many different varieties to choose from. Beetroot is versatile and can be eaten in salads, and as a side dish for all kinds or recipes, including meat and fish.

Soil

Beetroots need alkaline soil that is rich in nutrients with a little sand added to the mix. You need to regularly feed the plant once every six weeks or so.

Varieties

The varieties of beets for a small-space garden are boltardy, chiogga and cylindra. These varieties have narrow and long roots that need a deeper and not a wider pot. So, you can easily plant them in close quarters.

Common problems

The one that pest that you need to keep your eyes peeled for is Mangold fly and its young ones. This pest forms white tunnels on the surface of the leaf. If the leaves of beets turn yellow, then it indicates a nutrient-deficiency and implies that it is time to feed the plant.

Carrots

You need a variety that matures quickly and provides a good yield. Carrots are well suited for pots and can grow well in closed spaces. These plants make for a pretty sight when you plant them in terracotta pots. You cannot transplant carrots, so you need to directly sow them into the container you want them to grow in. They need a little warmth to grow. They can grow in shade as well, however, their growth will be a little slow.

Soil

Carrots have a high sensitivity to the soil. It must be loosely packed deep and fertile soil with plenty of sand. The ideal ratio of sand and compost is 40:60. Always add a little perlite to the pot and opt for a deep pot to accommodate the roots.

Varieties

The varieties of carrots ideal for a small space garden are Parisienne, Paris market and Caracas.

Common problems

If you notice reddish leaves, it indicates carrot fly. To prevent this, place the pots at least a meter off the ground since these flies fly close to the ground. During the growing period, ensure that you cover the top of the root is well covered with soil to prevent a green top.

Lettuce

Lettuces are easy to grow and you can pick leaves whenever you want to. They grow well even with close planting. There are four varieties of lettuces to choose from and these are loose-leaf, butterheads, crisp-heads and cos lettuce. The salad bowl is a good example of a loose-leaf lettuce and they form a tight head. Crisp heads have tight hearts and very crispy leaves like the iceberg lettuce. Butterhead lettuces have sweet-tasting and waxy-textured leaves. Whenever you pick the leaves, never pick more than 30-40% of the growth.

When you sow lettuce seeds, sow them at least one inch apart in 4-inch rows. You can harvest them in about 4 to 6 weeks. You need to cut the lettuce half an inch above the ground and allow the plant to regrow.

Soil

Lettuces need moist, alkaline and nutrient-rich soil. You can use loose compost of good quality with some lime mixed in. Add lime only when the soil isn't alkaline. The soil must always be moist as dry soil can kill the plant.

Varieties

The little gem, winter gem, salad bowl, Tom Thumb and lollo rosso are good small-space varieties.

Common problems

Pests seem to love lettuces. Since lettuce needs damp and moist soil to grow, it also attracts different fungi. If you notice any mold, you need to immediately remove the affected foliage to protect the healthy leaves. To prevent any pests from crawling up to the lettuce, place crushed eggshells around the plant. You can also use slug pellets and fine netting to prevent pests from feasting on the leaves.

Potatoes

Potatoes are quite easy to grow, and you can grow them all through summer and spring. There are small varieties of potatoes that are perfect for small-space gardening. You need to be careful when you buy the seeds and always buy certified seeds. You can harvest potatoes as soon as the first flush of flowers on the plant dies.

Soil

Potatoes are the least fussy of all plants. You can plant them in any soil. You simply need to mix a little manure with some multi-purpose compost before you plant them.

Varieties

Always opt for the early varieties of potatoes. This variety produces small plants that you can comfortably grow in pots and planters.

Common problems

Potatoes are usually pest-free. However, blight can at times attack the crop. At the first sign of blight, use some copper spray to remedy the issue.

Radishes

Radishes are quite easy to grow, and they mature quickly. Not just that, there are different small types of radishes that you can choose from. They can grow well in shade, but they thrive in sunlight.

Soil

Radishes aren't fussy about the soil type and can grow anywhere. However, if you want a healthy growth of radishes, ensure that the sand to compost ratio of the soil is 30:70.

Varieties

The best varieties of radish for small garden area are cherry belle and scarlet globe.

Common problems

You need to be wary of slugs and snails. However, pests aren't a common problem for radishes.

Pole Beans

Also known as green beans, they will make a great addition to your garden. You can grow them in pots with the support of stakes, in trellises or even out in the yard. They are easy to maintain and grow. They are resistant to a lot of diseases and give a good yield. Whenever you feel that the bean pods are firm and sizeable, simply break them off the plant.

Soil

Pole beans don't need any special type of soil, but they thrive in sandy soils. Cover the soil to keep it a little warm for the seeds to germinate. Beans cannot bear cold weather, so plant them accordingly. Sow the seeds 2 inches apart and don't ever plant them too close to one another. If you are not planting them in a vertical garden then beans require poles or stakes to grow up. Bamboo poles are best for this purpose. Don't forget to mulch the soil but do not over-fertilize it.

Varieties

The ideal varieties of beans for a small space garden are Kentucky wonder, fortex and bush blue lake.

Common problems

If the weather is too hot, then the plant will not bloom. Also, if the nitrogen content is too high in the soil, it will prevent the pods from growing. Excess nitrogen will give you a bushy plant but no flowers. Keep an eye out for aphids, mold and beetles. Use any organic pesticide of your choice to protect the bean plants.

Tomatoes

It is best suited to be grown during the hot months of summer. So, ensure that wherever you plan to plant tomatoes, that spot receives plenty of sunlight.

Soil-preference

Tomatoes are not fussy about the soil and they can pretty much grow in any soil condition. One thing that you must keep in mind is to regularly feed the plant once it starts flowering.

Varieties

The ideal varieties of tomatoes for a small garden are the F1 totem, Tommy toe and maskotka.

Common problem

Blight is a very common problem for tomatoes. To prevent blight, ensure that the water doesn't splash onto the foliage especially when you water the plant.

Strawberries

A bush of strawberries does make for a pretty sight. You can grow them quite easily in pots, provided the weather conditions are favorable.

Soil

Strawberries need sand to compost ratio of 30:70 to grow and thrive. The soil needs to be slightly acidic and not alkaline. So, you don't need to add any lime when you want to grow strawberries.

Varieties

You don't have to stick to a particular variety of strawberries and any variety will do well.

Common problem

The one thing that you need to be aware of is to prevent the fruit from coming in contact with the soil below. You do want to enjoy juicy strawberries, don't you? If yes, then ensure that the strawberries don't touch the soil. If it happens, the fruit will attract all sorts of pests and fungi.

Lemons

Lemons need fertile potting soil and always use natural fertilizers like compost and manure. The pot needs to be quite wide to accommodate lemon plants. A pot that is six inches deep and six inches wide can hold one tree. Lemons need a lot of sunlight to thrive, so pick a sunny spot. If you want, you can sow all the seeds in a huge planter and then transplant the seedlings into individual pots. Don't forget to water the plant regularly and feed the soil without fail. Lemons need slightly sandy and loamy soil to thrive. The best time to sow lemon is at the onset of spring.

Herbs

Herbs are very easy to tend to. However, you need to wait for a while before you can harvest the plant after you sow the seeds. Ensure that the soil isn't too damp when you sow the seeds. They need at least 6 hours of sunlight daily. Sufficient water and sunlight are all that herbs need to thrive. As soon as the weather turns cold, bring the herbs inside; they don't do well in the cold.

You can grow some simple herbs that you regularly use. You will need a steel tub that is galvanized. The tub must have holes that are drilled into its bottom. This facilitates in draining of water. You will need to pick up the required soil, seeds or seedlings, water and most important of all, sunlight! If you are fond of fresh herbs, then you can make your herb planter. You can grow all the herbs that you can think of in this planter. Basil, cilantro, parsley, coriander, dill, rosemary, thyme and even mint. It is advisable that you grow herbs like dill and mint in their containers. However, a couple of woody herbs like rosemary and thyme can be grown together as well. You can have your very own herb garden on your windowsill. How convenient is it? If you are interested in herbal teas, then you can grow peppermint, lemon balm, thyme, lemon verbena and something like chamomile in small pots in your home. You can pluck your fresh harvest in the summer and sun dry it so that you can also enjoy it in the winter.

CHAPTER FIVE:

Gardening Strategies

"Don't judge each day by the harvest you reap but by the seeds that you plant." – Robert Louis Stevenson.

Depending on the method of gardening you have chosen, you will have to select the produce that you want to grow. You can opt for the container, vertical, or raised bed gardening. Depending on this, there are different strategies that you can make use of for growing plants. You will need to select the right plants so that you can make most of the space that you have.

Companion planting

This requires a little research and a little through on which plants you personally prefer. There are some plants that are companionable and can be grown in close quarters. Then there are a few varieties that aren't suitable to be grown together. For instance, marigold and pole beans can be grown together. Here is a list of plants that make good companions and these are beans, carrots and squash, eggplants and beans, tomatoes and basil, lettuce and herbs, spinach and onions. Here are a few combinations that you must avoid and these are beans and onions/ garlic, carrots and fennel/ dill, onions and beans, onions and peas, tomatoes with squash, or tomatoes with potatoes.

Crop rotation

Most gardeners usually know that they must avoid growing the same crop more than once in the same year or at the same location. Especially if the crop belongs to the mustard family, you need to avoid this. If you decide to plant in containers, then you must certainly use new potting soil in every garden season. A systematic schedule ensures that every section of the container will receive each family of plants. There are four basic families when it comes to vegetables. Leafy plants, fruit, roots and legumes. The plants suitable for crop rotation are as follows:

- Leafy plants: Lettuce, cabbage, broccoli, spinach, Brussel sprouts and salad greens.

- Fruit: Tomatoes, peppers, corn, squash, potatoes, cucumbers, eggplant.

- Roots: Carrots, beets, radishes, onions and turnips.

- Legumes: Beans, peas, peanuts and cover crops.

During the first year, you can grow leaves, fruit, roots and legumes in this order in the four sections. The next year you will vary the order by growing fruit, roots, legumes and leaves. Keep doing this until all the combinations are exhausted.

Succession planting:

There are some plants that mature at a quicker pace when compared to others. A small-space garden can, therefore, be planted, harvested and replanted once again within the growing season. For succession planting, the best-suited crops are lettuce, radishes and green beans. Lettuce and tomatoes don't take long to mature, so you harvest these long before the tomato and pepper plants will take to fill up the available space. There are a few crops like spinach and broccoli that produce summer and fall harvest. You can fill up the space between the spring and fall time with crops that grow quickly, like carrots and radishes.

Intensive planting:

You can make the most of the space that is available to you by planting plants as close together as is possible without exhausting the soil. There won't be any vacant space for the growth of weeds when you follow this method of planting. Depending upon the size of the container and the raised bed, you can grow as many plants as you possibly can. Interplanting helps to make use of the space that is present next to a plant that will take a whole season to mature. There are a few plants that only take a little while to mature and these can be planted between slow-growing plants like eggplants, peppers and tomatoes. Early crops can be harvested before the slower ones. Salad greens, radishes and scallions can be made use of for interplanting.

Vertical gardening

Vegetables:

Climbing beans and tomatoes vines grow up in strings and can climb along fences. Cherry tomatoes, hot peppers also grow well in containers and are gorgeous to behold. Pole beans wrap themselves up along their nearest pole and will be perfect for vertical gardening. Cucumbers are vines as well and they can grow really well along with a fence. Squash tends to occupy a lot of space when grown at a ground level, but making use of trellises for growing them is certainly a good space saving idea. Growing vegetables that naturally grow in vines is a really good idea or you can grow plants that can thrive in small pots, like peppers.

Fruit:

For growing grapes, you will have to make use of a special layering technique and the same will be applicable for any espaliered fruit trees as well. This not difficult to master but it might be a better project to be taken on by an intermediate gardener than a beginner. So, if this is your first attempt at vertical gardening then you should stick to fruit that won't be too hard to grow vertically, like vines of strawberry and kiwis.

Flowers:

If you are looking for plants that will provide you with colorful flowers, then you can consider creeping phlox or morning glories. Lantana bushes can also be trained for growing off hanging planters. There are creeping varieties of nasturtiums and they can grow really well in vertical pockets. Nasturtiums are edible flowers!!

If you are making use of hanging planters or even vertical wall designs then you will need to make sure that you are using soil that's incredibly rich in nutrients and also that you are able to drain the soil well. It will mean that you will have to make use of rocks at the bottom so that the drainage holes stay clear and other media like coconut coir or peat moss can also make use of because they can absorb moisture and release it to the plant during the day. One of the problems that you will need to overcome with container planting is that the soil tends to dry up fast and you will need to keep watering it frequently. Nutrient depletion also occurs over time and you will need to either replace or replenish the soil that you are making use of for vertical gardening.

CHAPTER SIX:

Spend Less Time
Watering the Garden

"It will never rain more roses: when we want to have more roses, we must plant more trees."
— George Eliot

Most of us tend to have a time constraint these days. Watering the garden is an important aspect of gardening. However, there are a couple of things that you can do to spend less time watering the plants. In this chapter, you will learn about these solutions.

Harvest rainwater

The best way to harvest rainwater is to install a rain barrel and then reuse it for your garden. A rainwater collecting system is easy to install and it collects water from the home's gutters and uses the same to water the plants in a garden. Even a small rain barrel can harvest more than 30 gallons of water. Think of all the plants that you can water with 30 gallons of water or more! Why is rainwater harvesting good? Not only does it reduce your work, but it is environmentally friendly as well.

Link it up

If you want to save time, then it is a good idea to link the sprinkler system with an irrigation timer. It will automatically handle all the watering needs of your garden. You can control an irrigation time from your smartphone, tablet or even your desktop. For instance, Blossom is a good irrigation timer and it will save at least 30% of your water bill. A system like this pretty much pays for itself. The system will automatically program itself according to the local weather and create a watering schedule that is optimal. For instance, Blossom will provide extra water to the plants on the days that are quite sunny and dry, and on those days with a rain forecast, it will irrigate less.

Soak the roots

You can use a drip irrigation system or a soaking hose to water the plants. These tools help conserve water because they slowly deliver moisture only to the roots of the plants. Take a soaker hose and place it in the mulch around the plants. Once you do this, you merely need to turn the hose on and let it do its work. You can link the soaker hose and drip irrigation systems to a hose timer and let it do all your work.

Weather

Ensure that you check the weather updates regularly to check the probability of a rain. You can use an app on your smartphone or tablet to do this. The best time to water the plants is early in the morning before the heat of the day sets in.

Plan and plant

Before you plant the garden, take some time to plan the kind of plants you want. You can opt for plants that are drought-tolerant and need less water. You will not only save on watering the plants but also on the time needed for gardening. Select those plants that will thrive in the local soil time and place them in a space that has proper lighting.

Revamp the soil

You can conserve and retain moisture in the soil with a couple of products. Mulch is the best option that's available and it helps keep the soil moist even in sweltering heat. You can even use some water-storing crystals to reduce your work. When you water the plants, these crystals will absorb the moisture and then slowly release them to the roots of the plants. These crystals or mulch also prefer the plants from over or under-watering.

A watering wand

If you use containers, hanging baskets or window boxes, then you need a watering wand. A watering wand makes it easier to water all those plants in hard to reach places.

CHAPTER SEVEN:

Tools and Equipment

"Gardens are not made by 'singing oh, how beautiful,' and sitting in the shade." – Rudyard Kipling

Yes indeed. Gardening does not happen all by itself. It requires conscious and consistent efforts. In order to make the most of these efforts there are a couple of tools and equipment wich every gardener needs. In this section, you will learn about all this and more.

Gloves

Gloves aren't absolutely necessary. However, if you don't want any dirt getting stuck underneath your fingernails, then you need some gloves. Not just that, it is a good idea to wear gloves, especially when you mix fertilizers into the soil or when you spray organic insecticides on the plants. Apart from this, gloves also protect your hands from thorns and other sharp parts of a plant.

A watering can

You can either buy a watering can for your garden or make one out of an old milk jug. It helps transport water, especially if you don't want to buy a hose. Watering cans imitate the flow of trickling rainwater, instead of gushing water onto the plants. When you pour water on the plants, ensure that the water doesn't hit the soil and splashes back onto the foliage. When this happens, it can lead to the growth of fungus. To avoid all this, you need a watering can.

Spade, Fork and Trowel

If you have raised beds or a small outdoor garden, then you need a trowel and a fork. It helps to dig through the dirt and loosen up the soil a little. You can always use your hands to do this, but it is so much easier when you have a trowel to help you along. If you

Pruners

You need to prune the plants regularly. Pruning means cutting dead foliage off the plants. You might wonder why you need pruners when you can use scissors for the same. Well, plants have wet sap and when you cut the foliage, the sticky residue can make the scissors sticky. To avoid all this, it is a good idea to buy a good pair of pruners.

Organic pesticides

Regardless of how careful you are with your garden, pests are something that you cannot avoid. You need to keep some organic pesticide on hand. Mix it with water in a spraying can and spray it on your plants regularly. Spray this mixture on your plants at least once a month to prevent any potential pest invasion.

String and sticks

If you want to grow plants in a container, then you need some sticks and yarn to support the growth of the plants. For instance, if you want to grow tomatoes in a pot, then the young plant will need some support to grow well. Place a stick in the soil and wind up some soft yarn around the plant and the stick to give it the necessary support.

CHAPTER EIGHT:

About Fertilization and Drainage

"Fertilizer does no good in a heap, but a little spread around works miracles all over." –
Richard Brinsley Sheridan

Fertilization

If you are planting in either pots or boxes, then you can use a potting mix as soil. Black earth or something like the triple mix will prove to be too dense for plants in a pot. The potting mix will be an ideal one for gardening on balconies. If you plan on growing edible varieties, then it is better to make use of organic fertilizers instead of the synthetic ones.

Have you ever wondered what all those numbers on a package of fertilizer are? They represent the composition or the levels of Nitrogen, Phosphorus and Potassium. These three nutrients help in the upward, downward and the flowering growth of a plant. When you are growing any vegetables or herbs, that have a very short growing season, you will need something that will promote the development of fruit or flowers, along with upwards growth. Therefore, you must pick up a fertilizer that has got high first and last numbers.

When a plant starts growing, the intensive process of growth drains the soil of all its nutrients. Adding some fertilizer will help in replenishing the soil once again. Selecting the right type of fertilizer and the quantity to be used will depend on the type of the soil and the kind of plants that you plan on growing. Why don't we get started with deciphering the numbers we were talking about earlier?

All the commercial fertilizers have a label with three numbers that represent the ratio of nutrients present in it. For instance, 12-12-12, 5-5-5. 5-10-5, and 4-12-0. The first number represents the percentage of Nitrogen, the second one stands for Phosphate and the third one for Potash. For instance, a fertilizer with the numbers 5-10-5 consists of 5% nitrogen, 10% phosphate and 5% Potash. A fertilizer with all the three nutrients is referred to as a complete fertilizer. A bone meal, on the other hand, will have no potash.

An example of it is a fertilizer with a composition of 4-12-0. There are three numbers that are printed on every bag or even a bottle of fertilizer. These numbers are always in the same order and it represents the percentage according to their weight. The order is NPK and it stands for Nitrogen, Phosphorus and Potassium. Each of these ingredients is necessary for the growth of the plant. For instance, if you pick up a bag of an all-purpose organic fertilizer, it will carry the numbers 5-5-5.

The first number represents Nitrogen. Nitrogen is essential for the growth of the plant's health. It is responsible for the lush green growth of a plant. So, a nitrogen-rich fertilizer is the best choice for a leafy vegetable like lettuce or Swiss chard. The natural sources of nitrogen are feather meal and liquid fish emulsion. The second number stands for the content of Phosphorus. Phosphorus is responsible for the healthy roots of a plant and is especially important for the development of fruit and flowers. This is essential for blooming plants like tomatoes, bell peppers or any peppers and other ornamental plants. Organic sources of phosphorus are bone meal and seabird guano. The third number in the sequence stands for Potassium. This is essential for the development of the stem and the overall strength of the plant. Root crops like carrots, potatoes and beets require a potassium-rich fertilizer. Also, young trees require this. A natural source of potassium is palm bunch ash, and sulfate of potash magnesia. Plants are capable of absorbing nutrients not just through their roots but through the pores present in their leaves as well. Foliar feeding is the process of supplying nutrients to the plant through the leaf pores. This can be done by applying or sprinkling a fertilizer solution on the plant. It is effective for enhancing the growth of the plants and gives them an additional boost. Now that you understand what these numbers mean, you will need to choose between an organic and a chemical fertilizer.

Organic fertilizers

You can use organic fertilizer to maintain a beautiful garden and obtaining wonderful produce. Organic fertilizers comprise animal manure, green manure, blood meal, fish emulsion and rock phosphate as well as cottonseed meal. Organic fertilizers have got various advantages. Most of the organic fertilizers help in improving the soil structure by improving the microbe and nutritional content. It helps in providing a steady but slow supply of nutrition to the plant. Organic fertilizers like manure or compost can be made at home and it is very cheap. There are complete organic fertilizers available in the market like the 5-5-5 and these are the best alternatives to chemical fertilizers available in the market.

Chemical fertilizers

All the chemical fertilizers are manufactured synthetically. The elements included in this are sodium nitrate, potassium chloride and super-phosphate. These are available in liquid, pellet, powder and even granular form as well. You can fertilize your plants while watering them by mixing up some liquid fertilizer in the watering can. If you are making use of the granular form of fertilizer, then you can sprinkle this around the plant. Chemical fertilizers are easily available, they aren't expensive, and are quick acting as well. However, there are several disadvantages of making use of such chemical fertilizers. Chemical fertilizers don't add any organic matter to the soil and they don't help in improving the soil structure. In fact, they damage the microorganism present in soil and make the soil unfit in the long run. Think of chemical fertilizers as vitamin supplements instead of a nourishing meal. The manufacturing of chemical fertilizers requires the usage of non-renewable resources. This process contributes towards an increase in the carbon footprint.

Drainage

It might sound like common advice, and it holds true for only pots that haven't got any holes in it. If you are placing a container plant inside a larger pot, then in such a case you can place some kind of coarse material in the bottom of the outer pot. Doing this will ensure that the roots of the plant are kept out of any excess water. If you want to make sure that the plant roots don't rot when you are directly planting in the larger container, then in such a case place some gravel at the bottom. You need to keep an important point in your mind while doing this. If a pot has holes, then placing gravel in it does no good. Water will naturally flow towards the finer material. This means that water won't escape from the space present in between the gravel. The gravel will simply help in making sure that the soil isn't exiting the pot. Always make use of a good potting mix for ensuring good drainage. Garden soil is too dense for potting and isn't suitable, therefore.

One common mistake that a lot of people commit while watering their plants, they tend to wash them as well. People tend to pour water on top of the plant. If the plant leaves are left wet for a long time, it attracts pests and diseases. Always make sure that the water touches the soil and this will help the roots in absorbing the moisture.

CHAPTER NINE:

General Gardening Tips for Busy People

"A garden is a grand teacher. It teaches careful watchfulness; it teaches industry and thrift; above all it teaches entire trust." – Gertrude Jekyll

It is no secret that everybody is busy these days and hardly finds time to do what they love. Gardening after a long day can feel tiresome and often make people lose interest, but some of the best gardeners in the world are busy people.

Do not let others tell you how good a gardener you are. It is all about being satisfied with what you do and enjoying your passion. There will be some experts out there telling you that it is important to pay attention to your garden every day, but this is not true. Gardening can be rewarding even if you spend only a little time doing it.

Busy people can break rules

Well, there are no set rules and you can make and break them as you wish. There is no rule that says your garden has to be trim and neat all the time. It will only be important if your plants are suffering and there are too many weeds growing.

You might have to cut back on some of the crops and get each one of those weeds out to make sure the garden is doing well.

How often you pull them out is up to you but will be advisable to do so often to make sure the garden is maintained well. Do not make it all about the weekends and try to garden in the evenings when you come home from work. It can be quite therapeutic and you will be satisfied that you do not have to push all the work to the weekends. It is all about doing a little at a time and getting your hands dirty to keep your precious garden looking nice. It can give you a good workout if you get in there and do the job wholeheartedly. Make sure you have all the tools and equipment handy so that you can begin work as soon as you can and place the tools back so that they are easily accessible next time.

Entertainment

Do not forget to enjoy your gardening experience. Be it playing the radio or having your headphones on, music can enhance your gardening experience. Tune into your favorite songs and go about trimming those bushes and plucking those tomatoes!

Company

Make sure you have good company when you are gardening. It can be your neighbor to chitchat with, your toddler who wants to learn gardening or even your dog! Dogs love spending time in the garden and will love to keep you company as you go about tidying the garden. Some people go for hens or cocks too as they too can serve as great garden pets and keep the garden in good shape by eating pests.

Schedule it

Make a list of things that have to be done in the garden as otherwise, it will be difficult to go about your chores. It can save a lot of time and energy if you know exactly what needs attention. Right from trimming to watering to adding fertilizer to cutting the plants, make sure you have a list ready and also mention the times when they have to be performed, and a note of by what time you need to finish. Spend your spare time thinking what you can do to enhance your garden and make it work for you.

Remember that there is a right time and place for everything. This extends to your garden and the plants in it. Make sure you are doing the right things in the garden at the right time of year to enhance its appeal and make sure your plants are healthy.

Get over failure

Not all crops will turn out the way you want them to. Some will excel in bad conditions while some will do badly in good conditions. It is difficult to predict how plants will do despite good care. Whether it is a bad crop or your favorite herb plant that has died, it will be important to move forward instead of being discouraged.

Future planning

If you are going for a full-fledged garden then make sure you plan well into the future. It will take some level of planning to ensure that the garden can grow out to its full extent and is not restricted in any way. This is especially important if you are going for perennial crops, as it will not be easy for them to adjust to conditions all year round. If you have a terrace garden then it will be even more important to plan it out and make sure the garden is placed correctly in the right confines. Since you will be busy, you must make sure everything is handy so that it is easy to carry out gardening.

Structure

It is important to get the structure right as it can help gardeners who have a time crunch. If you do not have the time to cater to your garden's needs every now and then, then it can lead to an overgrowth of weed and other uninvited plants and pests, but if the structure is such that the garden can be easily maintained without much effort with proper hedging and dedicated areas for different crops, then it will be easy to prune and maintain the garden. Invest in self-care plants that will not make a mess and are easy to maintain.

Rustic look

Busy people will accept it even if their gardens are a little messy as it can lend it a rustic look. If you are going for it then don't bother trimming the bushes and pulling out some of the weeds. Leave some back in a way that adds to the garden's look.

Get help

Get your family involved as much as possible. They should be available hands on to help you out, as you can be quite busy. Right from kids to your partner to siblings, everybody has to chip in as it will be your family garden and will provide for everyone. Assign them weekly tasks and reward them with a fresh fruit or vegetable from the garden.

CHAPTER TEN:

Hydroponics

"The best place to find god is in the garden. You can dig for him there." – George Bernard Shaw

Hydroponics is a unique concept that is ideal for all those who do not want to get their hands dirty in the soil. It is a great way to have a garden of your own without the hassle of dirt and soil.

But hydroponics is not for everyone. Even though it might sound like it is easy to have a hydroponics garden, it takes a lot of effort to own and maintain one. You have to decide whether you can manage a hydroponics garden depending on how busy you are and how much time can be spent maintaining the garden.

What is hydroponics?

Hydroponics is a style of gardening where plants are grown without soil. The term hydroponics stands for soil-less growing. The water used is not plain water, but nutrient rich water that contains everything plants need to be healthy. It can also contain perlite and sand as they are often found in regular soil.

Is hydroponics tough to maintain?

No, it does not have to be tough to maintain if you set it up correctly. In fact, it can prove to be child's play as all it takes is a little pruning to maintain the garden in top shape. It is a very basic concept where plants are suspended in nutrient rich water that has all the makings for plants growing long and strong. I'm sure you remember poking seeds with a toothpick and suspending them from a glass of water for the roots to stick out. The same concept holds true for hydroponics.

How to get started?

All you need is a hydroponics system along with hydroponic nutrients and hydroponics medium along with a little light, healthy plant cut offs and some spare time.

What is a hydroponics system?

The hydroponics system consists of a few standard structures including a tray that holds the nutrient rich water and the growing media for the plants. The system mainly has two components namely a liquid culture solution and an aggregate solution. In the solution system, the plant grows its roots directly into the solution containing the nutrients. In the aggregate system, there will be sand, gravel and pellets that will form the growing structure for the plant's roots. Both systems should ensure that the three main requirements of the plant are supplied including water, oxygen and nutrients.

There are different types of systems to pick from depending on the conditions that are available at your place. These include ebb and flow, drip system and nutrient film. Wick and Aeroponics systems are also good options to choose from.

Where can I buy hydroponics system?

Hydroponics systems can be bought commercially from suppliers. A simple Internet search will tell you who is selling hydroponic kits in your area. If there is no one available then consider looking it up on online sites. Ensure that the site is trustworthy and go through genuine testimonials to know whether they are the best choice. Ask them if they will be sending personnel from their end to set up the systems.

Can I build my own hydroponics system?

If you are capable then consider building the systems yourself. It will be easy to set it up if you have a handy instructional guide. It is all about connecting pipes and making sure the water flows out evenly. It will be advantageous to build your own systems as you can tweak it around to suit your needs.

What about nutrients and the medium?

Nutrients are the most important part of hydroponics and essential that you use the right type. Use a mixture of primary, secondary and micronutrients that are meant specifically for hydroponics. These nutrients can differ from system to system and you must come up with a mixture that suits your specific category of hydroponics system. If this is your first-time using hydroponics, then make sure it is kept simple and not too complicated as that overwhelm you. Use a popular formula that can be bought from a reliable supplier.

Apart from the water, the hydroponics medium can also contain clay pellets, perlite, coconut fiber or cocopeat, sand, vermiculture, etc. These structures should be solid and not easily break up or dissolve in the water medium. They have to absorb some of the nutrients so that they can be slowly released into the water. You can decide which medium you wish to use in your systems, but make sure the medium is not constantly wet as that can negatively impact root health.

What about pumps?

Air pumps should be added to the water to circulate oxygen and keep it airy. These systems dissolve bubbles into the water and supply oxygen to the roots. Air pumps are a must for all hydroponics systems.

How about light?

Hydroponics mostly makes use of artificial lights that contain metal halide. These are ideal as they can produce the ideal light for plants, but they tend to heat up faster and thus if you have the budget for it then go for LED lights as they will not heat up as much and produce the right amount of light.

Can I set up hydroponic gardens outdoors?

Yes. Hydroponic gardens will do well in the outdoors just as they would indoors. All it needs is the right medium and surroundings and natural light.

How long does the system take to produce plants?

As is the case with most gardens, the hydroponics system can take a little time to bloom. If you are new to the system, then it will take a little time for you to understand how it works. It will take time to set up the system. You will then have to pick the right plants to be grown under the right settings. Then, you will have to wait for the plants to grow out. This can take a good 2 to 3 months.

Is hydroponics organic?

It can be if you use organic fertilizers in the systems. Most systems do not automatically encourage use of organic fertilizers, but you have the option of using it. The lack of soil ecosystem does not make it any less organic than a traditional organic garden.

What plants can I grow through the system?

The system can be used to grow just about any kind of plant. Whatever can grow in a regular garden can most definitely grow in a hydroponics garden. Using the best solution for the garden will ensure that plants grow well. Right from cruciferous vegetables such as spinach, lettuce, kale to herbs, a variety of vegetables and fruit can be grown in the hydroponics system. The aggregate system works best for vegetables with deep roots like squash and cucumbers.

Does the yield slow down?

Not at all. The yield using hydroponics systems is usually much faster than traditional systems.

What will the crop taste like?

The crop will be excellent in taste. There is no reason for it to taste different or worse than traditionally grown produce. As the plants are getting all the same nutrients through the water the taste and quality remains very good.

CHAPTER ELEVEN:

Herbs for the Garden

"I know that if odor were visible, as color is, I'd see the summer garden in rainbow clouds."
— *Robert Bridges*

Basil

Sweet basil is a must for your garden as the smell alone can leave you feeling heady. It has a sweet anise seed like flavor but a strong aroma. Both dried and fresh basil are used in cuisine around the world. Just a little can go a long way in inducing a strong flavor. It is also used as a deodorizer and an anti-oxidant that can induce anti-inflammatory benefits. The herb is also a strong insect repellent and thus, will help to take care of the little pests around the garden. Basil is also a mouth freshener and contains vitamins A, K and C as well as magnesium, potassium and calcium.

It is easy to grow basil plants from its seed. Best time to plant will be early spring as the plant can be transplanted outdoors two weeks after frost has passed. It is also easy to grow the plant from clippings. Simply remove fresh but mature stocks from your existing lot or get them from a nursery and poke them into the soil.

It takes the seeds five to ten days to germinate and plants will need full morning sun and some degree of afternoon shade. The soil should be rich and moist and well-draining with a pH of 6 to 7. Add a fertilizer in the ratio of 2:1:1 with high nitrogen and add it every two weeks. Allow a spacing of 12 to 18 inches and harvest the herbs at ten weeks.

Chives

Chives are like onion and garlic plants and are a great investment if you wish to drive out pesky pests from your garden. Chives are rich in sulfur, which is a strong antibiotic. It imparts anti-inflammatory properties when consumed.

Both dried and fresh chives are great additions to recipes and are best served with meat dishes and potatoes.

It is best to grow chives from their seeds by sowing them directly into the soil and transplanting the plants outdoors in fall. Make sure you divide them from time to time to prevent clumping. To keep them fresh, make an effort to cut them fully from the base and leave just a half-inch stub in the ground. Removing the leaves will encourage the plant to grow bushier.

The seeds will germinate in two weeks and will require full sun with partial shade. The soil has to be rich and moist and well draining. Add compost that is nutritious and well balanced every three to four weeks. Maintain a spacing of four to eight inches for best results.

Cilantro

Cilantro is high in antioxidants and vitamin C and also contains several minerals. It is a refreshing herb the helps with digestion and can reduce inflammation in the body that can lead to gastric issues. Cilantro is better known as coriander in Asian countries and positively impacts blood sugar levels. It helps to reduce stress on the liver and pancreas and promotes insulin. Cilantro is predominantly used to flavor meat dishes and curries. It has anti-bacterial properties and is consumed to relieve flu symptoms.

Cilantro is very easy to grow and requires sowing of seeds directly in the outdoors. Cilantro can be a little too sensitive and requires a little extra care. All you have to do is scatter a few seeds all over wet soil and cover with about an inch of soil on top. Water regularly and plants will start to poke out within a couple of weeks. It can also be grown directly using plant stems. Just poke a healthy plant stem and a new plant will start to come up.

The plants can be prone to fungal infections and thus it would be best to clean and tidy the plants from time to time. They tend to attract aphids so keep the surroundings clean.

It takes about 10 days for the seeds to germinate and the plants require full sun. The soil has to be well draining with a pH of 6.2 to 6.8. Add a fertilizer once a month. It takes around a month for the plants to mature.

Lavender

Lavender is a fragrant herb that has medicinal properties. It releases natural oils that are of therapeutic uses. It is often used in cooking, especially for baking. Lavender can serve as a natural remedy to keep bugs and mosquitoes away.

Lavender can be grown from seeds indoors before transplanting them outdoors. Early spring is the best time to do so. Lavender requires moderate temperatures and cannot tolerate too much moisture or humidity. Thus, it is best to sow them in containers where the moisture is easy to control.

Lavender produces blooms during the summer. To encourage the plants to produce blooms, cut them from time to time and prune the leaves.

The seeds take 14 days to produce blooms and require full sun. The plant does well in well-draining soil that is a little sandy. Mid fall is the best time to sow the seeds. Maintain a space of 4 inches between the plants.

Lemon Balm

Lemon balm is a strong herb with a strong flavor and smell. It can provide a lot of health benefits and add a citrusy aroma to meals. It helps to relieve tension and stress and is used to find relief from muscle aches and pains. A fresh poultice can be used to heal a wound and cold sore. When consumed, lemon balm can help to relieve gas and stomach upsets. Lemon balm tea is widely consumed and can provide immunity and maintain mental health. The leaves are often chopped and added to salads.

It is easy to grow the lemon balm from the seeds and it is best to sow it indoors. Once the plants start to poke out, they have to be transplanted outdoors. It is easy to grow it using fresh stems, but wait for frost to pass before transplanting the plants into the soil. If the plants are already outside then make sure it is properly mulched so that frost does not affect the roots.

It takes about 14 days for the seeds to germinate. The plant requires full sun and afternoon shade. The soil should be rich, moist and well-draining. Maintain a pH between 6 and 7. Add a balanced nutrient mix consisting of high nitrogen and blood meal. The plants can grow to a height of 26 inches. Maintain a distance of 4 inches between the plants. They can be harvested at any time of the season.

Oregano

Oregano leaves are predominantly used to treat illnesses related to the respiratory tract and aids in digestion and parasitic infections. It is also useful in treating fungal infections. Applying a layer of oregano on the scalp can help to provide relief from dandruff. It can also serve as a natural bug repellent. It is best to sow the seeds indoors first and then transplant it outdoors after frost has passed. Cover it with mulch to keep the roots from freezing. It takes the plants 14 days to germinate. The plants need full sun preferably in the morning and some afternoon shade. Add a high nitrogenous fertilizer at the beginning. The plants should have a spacing of 12 inches. Harvest it in about 13 weeks.

Parsley

Parsley is a popular herb that is used as a topping for most curries. It can help to neutralize bad breath and keep the immune system strong. It has both anti-bacterial and anti-inflammatory properties. It is consumed to cleanse the systems and detoxify it. Parsley is consumed to balance out hormones and normalize hormone function. It is best to grow the seeds by sowing them indoors before moving the plants outdoors. The soil has to be moist and mulched regularly to keep frost away. If you want the plant to produce thinner leaves then prune it regularly and remove any thick stems that might be growing. Collect seeds from the plant to regrow new ones. Use a natural insecticide of neem oil and warm water to treat insects such as black swallowtail larvae as the plant is susceptible to its infestation. The plants take 30 days to germinate and require full sun and partial shade. The soil should be well draining and maintain a pH level of 6.7. It is best to add a balanced fertilizer containing nitrogen. Maintain a spacing of 18 inches between the plants for ideal growth. The plants can be harvested in 11 weeks.

Peppermint

Peppermint is a great herb to use to repel insects and pests. It has a strong flavor that can deter rats and rodents and control ant growth. It is also best to keep spiders away. It is mostly used as an herbal remedy for sinus infections and headaches and can help you relax after a long day. The herb can be used to remain alert and aids with menstrual cramps. It is also used to treat IBS.

Peppermint can be used in both savory and sweet dishes. Adding just a sprig of peppermint to sweet dishes can help to enhance the flavor. Mint leaves are predominantly used as a flavoring for drinks. Cut up a few leaves and add to water to make fruit infused water.

The plants can be grown by sowing the seeds indoors, then wait for the plant to poke out before transplanting it. Germinate the seeds by soaking them and then plant them into starters. This can take up to two weeks. The plants have to be covered with about two inches of mulch to keep them from frost.

Remember that peppermint can be quite invasive and end up growing like a weed. So, make sure you keep an eye on it and trim it regularly. It takes the plant about 15 days to germinate and the plants require full sun with a little afternoon shade. The soil has to be well draining and damp. Add a nitrogen rich fertilizer on a regular basis. Maintain a spacing of 18 inches between the plants. The plans can be harvested anytime during the growing season.

Rosemary

Rosemary is a popular herb predominantly used in Italian cuisine. The herb can be grown to keep away pests and insects. It is understood that the herb also repels cats. The strong pungent smell of Rosemary can be quite overbearing and spread throughout the garden. It is a natural remedy for stomach ailments and can be consumed to treat bad breath. The herb is also used to relieve aches and pains. Rosemary infused oil can be used to treat skin infections and control dandruff. It is also used to promote the growth of new hair. When ingested, rosemary can help to control stress and tension. The dried and fresh herbs are used in cuisine.

The plants can be grown from seeds indoors and then transplanted outdoors. Germinate the seeds and then plant them in starters. It is best to transplant them in spring, but the rate of germination can be low. It is easy to grow them from clippings. It is best to add a thick layer of mulch to protect the plants from frost. The seeds take 21 days to germinate. The plants need full sun to bloom. The soil has to be well draining and at a pH of 6 to 7. Apply a balanced fertilizer in spring. Maintain a spacing of 36 inches between the plants. The plants will be ready to harvest in 14 weeks.

Sage

Sage is an herb that has several medicinal properties. It is an effective herb that is used to reverse fevers and induce anxiety. It is ideal to treat nerve disorders. It is usually used to infuse in teas to treat stomach ailments and throat infections. The herb is used in both dried and fresh form in cooking. It has a mild citrusy taste. The flowers of the plant are also edible. It is predominantly used to season meat dishes and salads and herbal teas.

It is easy to grow the plants directly from the seeds after germination. The plants can also be transplanted using cuttings. It is ideal to lightly harvest the plant in the first year of growth to maintain root health. The flowers might drop or can be plucked during the early stages to help the plant grow stronger. Sage should be pruned regularly to keep the plant healthy. The seeds can take 21 days to germinate and the plants need full sun and afternoon shade. The soil should be well draining and slightly sandy. The pH should be maintained between 6.5 and 7. Incorporate organic fertilizers to keep the plants healthy. There should be a spacing of 12 inches between the plants. The plants will be ready to harvest in 13 weeks.

Tarragon

Tarragon is a good source of minerals and vitamins that are essential for good health. This includes iron, magnesium, zinc and different vitamins such as A and C. It also contains calcium required to maintain bone and teeth health. The leaves have antibacterial and anti-fungal properties that make it ideal to kill surface germs. It is used to make teas to provide relief from stomach issues. The oil extracted from tarragon is used as a natural deodorizer. Tarragon has an anise like flavor and is predominantly used to flavor soups and curries. It is used to sprinkle over salads to add a citrusy flavor.

It is easy to grow tarragon plants from seeds and can be propagated indoors. They can then be transplanted outdoors. It is easy to grow the plants from cuttings. It is best to grow this herb in pots, as it will be easier to trim and maintain. Don't worry if the plants have died down in winter, as they will begin to grow back in spring. The seeds take 14 days to germinate and require sun with partial afternoon shade. The soil needs to be well draining. The plants do not require much fertilizer to do well. The plants should be placed at a spacing of 18 inches. They can be harvested in 11 weeks.

Thyme

Thyme is a good source of antioxidants and is good for eyes, skin and hair. It has anti-inflammatory properties and is used as an antibiotic. It is also known for its antiseptic properties. Consuming thyme infused tea can be beneficial to fight colds and sore throats. Thyme oil is used to treat acne and skin disorders. Rinse your scalp using thyme on a regular basis to treat dandruff. It can also be used to treat dry scalp. Thyme is used to flavor curries and soups. It can also be used to add to sauces. It is often used to flavor pizzas. It can add a woody texture to the dish.

It is best to grow thyme from seed by sowing it indoors and then transplanting it outdoors after frost has passed. Early spring is best to sow the plants. Thyme is used as an ornamental plant as it can creep around the garden. This plant can invite pollinators such as bees. It is best to prune the plants in spring, as it will encourage better growth. Pinch the new leaves back to help the plants grow bushier. The seeds take 21 days to germinate. The plants will need light sun and partial shade. The soil should be well draining and have a pH level of 7. This plant does not need fertilizers. Maintain a spacing of 8 inches between the plants. Harvest them after 14 weeks.

CHAPTER TWELVE:

Fruit for the Garden

"Cooking and gardening involve so many disciplines: math, chemistry, reading, history." – *David Chang*

Strawberries

Strawberries are amazing container plants and can grow in a host of conditions. They are the perfect home garden fruit plants and are perennial. This means that you only have to plant them once. They can be brought indoors during winter to protect from frost.

A good variety of strawberries to choose are the ever bearing, which can give you two harvests in a single year. The first one will be in June and the second in late summer.

Bear in mind that the container has to be at least 18 inches wide to help the plants grow out properly and the soil needs to be well draining. Expose the plants to about eight hours of direct sun for best results.

Blueberries

Blueberries can make excellent companions to your strawberry plants, but they will need a little more love and care. Use a pot that is at least 22 inches wide and 18 inches deep as this gives the plant enough space to grow out. The soil has to be acidic in nature and preferably contain peat. The plants will bloom from June until August. It can take at least two seasons for the plants to produce good crop.

Figs

Figs can sound a bit random to be grown in containers, but they can be quite a good option for a small garden. The pot has to be at least 16 inches wide. The soil should be well draining. They will need full sun and daily watering, especially during the hot months. They might need support to grow out effortlessly. Be gentle while plucking the fruit. It can take them at least three seasons to produce healthy fruit.

Tomatoes

Tomatoes are usually considered a fruit although they are mostly used in savory dishes. Tomatoes are extremely easy to grow in containers. Get a good variety and simply scatter the seeds all over the pot and cover with an inch of topsoil. Water regularly and wait at least a month for the plants to reach a good height before taking out the weaker plants. The plants might need support but make sure you add it early on to avoid damaging the roots.

Pineapple

Now you may wonder if it is possible to grow pineapples in a container and the answer is yes! All you have to do is cut off the crown of a pineapple and soak it in water for a couple of days. Plant it in a large enough container and place it under full sun. In no time, you will have a brand new, homegrown pineapple.

Musk melon

Better known as a cantaloupe, a muskmelon is an amazing summer fruit. Their fresh taste can be extremely appetizing and leave you wanting more, but the pot you use to grow this plant will have to be quite big, but make sure you use a support or trellis to lend the plant enough support to grow out properly. They will grow as vines. Do not worry if the vines droop down to support the fruits. They can handle the weight.

Bananas

Bananas are a great option as container plants only if the container is large enough. They are perennial plants and thus, it is fine to simply plant them once. They can be brought indoors to keep them from frost. These plants need a large container that can support the entire plant. The plants need full sun and regular watering to produce fruits, but make sure you do not over crowd containers and limit it to just one plant per pot. The plant might take a good two to three seasons to produce the best fruits.

Watermelon

Watermelons can be a good choice to grow in containers but only if you pay good attention to it. This means it needs proper watering and full sun. It also requires proper support, especially for the vines that will bear the fruit. Again, do not worry if the vines stoop down, they will be capable of supporting the fruits. These plants do well when planted on the ground. If you do not have space in your outdoor garden for this plant then consider planting it indoors. It will require well-draining soil. Artificial light will be a must, especially one that focuses on this plant. Although watermelons are supposed to be seasonal, some varieties can produce fruits all year round.

Currants

Black currants are good home garden plants packed with nutrition. Most people would not typically go for these, as they are quite uncommon, but having them in your garden can be quite rewarding. They will need a large container and lots of water. They also need full sun to produce the fruit. The compost has to be mixed with dirt and fertilizers. They will need adequate support, especially during growing season.

Gooseberries

Gooseberries are a good fruit option for your house garden. They are ideal plants for container gardening, especially if you have limited space available. Gooseberries are packed with nutrition and a rich source of vitamin C. it is very easy to grow them from seed. Simply cut open a fruit and remove the seed. Pierce toothpicks and suspend it in a glass of water. Change the water every few days. Once the roots start to grow out, plant them in a large enough container and allow the plants to grow out. The fruits will be ready to harvest in about a year's time.

Oranges

Oranges can be grown in containers provide the containers are big enough. It might take the tree about three years to start producing fruits but the time and dedication will be well worth it. You will fall in love with this plant as not only will it produce sweet and brightly colored oranges but also spread an amazing aroma all through the garden. Consider starting them from seeds indoors before planting them outdoors. Remember that it will be difficult to transplant these once they are in their containers. So, choose their spots carefully before planting them.

Lemons

Lemons are an amazing choice and can produce amazing little fruit. Lemons will produce quite a lot of fruit if they are placed in the right location and under the right conditions. They might, however, drop their first set of flowers as the plant can find it difficult to hold on to them while strengthening its roots. The plant needs well-draining soil and full sun.

Mulberries

Mulberries are great for small gardens. They can grow well in well-draining soil and will require full sun. Once they start growing, they will require little to no care. The dwarf varieties will do well in smaller gardens or container gardening, but make sure you pluck the ripe fruits as soon as they ripen and do not allow them to fall off as that can stain the places where they fall.

Passion Fruit

Passion fruit are extremely beautiful and produces sweet tasting fruits that are unique in structure. The plants will need quite a lot of space to grow out. It requires the right weather conditions to grow and thus, make sure you plant them in well-draining soil and place the plants under full sun. Passion fruits can be grown directly from seeds. They can produce fruits during late summer. Be gentle while dealing with them and make sure you do not pluck the fruits with too much force.

Container Gardening Tips

- Container gardening can be quite rewarding and pretty much need the same care and attention as regular gardens. Invest in a few good containers that are hardy and can help you grow tall and healthy plants
- Containers will need just as much sun as regular plants unless you plan to sow indoor plants

- The containers should be well-draining so that the water does not get logged

- It is extremely important to feed your plants a good fertilizer from time to time to ensure that they have access to all the important nutrients. They will not be in direct ground, which means they cannot access the right nutrients to grow healthy plants. Thus, add a good fertilizer regularly

- It is quite obvious that the size of the container will depend on the size of the plant. Large plants will need large containers and smaller plants will need smaller containers

- It would be ideal to add about four plants in a single pot by maintaining at least 4 inches space between each. Over crowding can lead to plants that are not healthy and produce mediocre fruit

- If you plan to plant in containers then get potting soil that is the best in the market. It should be well draining and also contain important nutrients required to produce healthy plants

- It is important to know what plants should be planted next to each other. Some plants love to have specific neighbors. For example, lemon plants will love to be next to orange trees. Both the plants will do well as they will prefer each other's company

- Do not worry if you do not find success with some of the plants. You cannot always successfully grow plants. If some have not done well then remove them and plant another in its place

- Go for plants that are meant to be specifically grown in your areas. This will make it easier to grow and maintain the plants

- Be careful with how much you water container plants. Place pebbles at the bottom to control humidity

CHAPTER THIRTEEN:

Indoor Plants for Busy People

"I love things that are indescribable, like the taste of an avocado or the smell of a gardenia."
— Barbara Streisand

Do not limit yourself to just an outdoor garden and consider having an indoor one as well. It is quite easy to start an indoor garden if you know what to grow. It can also be rewarding as it can spruce up your space and add a touch of elegance to your indoors.

Here is a selection of indoor plants that can be easily grown indoors by busy people.

Lucky Bamboo

Lucky bamboo is alternately known as Chinese bamboo and will make an excellent addition to any room. The plant is quite hardy and a good choice for both houses and offices. It is important to look for a plant that is healthy and has dark green shoots and leaves. It is extremely easy to care for these plants and will grow without soil in just a bowl of fresh water. They are easily available and can be found in nurseries and also grocery stores.

Pothos

Pothos refers to money plant and is the perfect houseplant. It requires medium sunlight and the perfect plant for those who usually forget to water their plants.

It is the best plant to go for if you are just starting out with gardening. These plants can purify the air around them, which is the plants best feature.

Peace lily

Peace lilies are beautiful indoor plants that can brighten up any space. It will do well in a room that gets indirect light. Do not be too generous with the watering and only water the soil once the top layer starts to look dry. Mist the plant every now and then using water without any chlorine in it. If the plant has developed any browning leaves then cut it to help the plant do well. The plant produces special white leaves that look like flowers.

Cacti

Cacti are great houseplants. They are succulents that can be divided into stem succulents, caudiciform succulents and leafy succulents. A lot of indoor cacti are stem succulents. They are usually distinct to look at with a cushion like structure on top of their stems that are known as areolas and have thorns and fine hair. They will develop flowers on top and all over the shoots. Cacti are the perfect houseplants for anyone looking for a very low maintenance plant around the house. They will do well in a host of climates but prefer dry and arid. They will do well indoors without water for four months. The pot should have a good drainage system in place and it is best to water the plants from the bottom up. A good way of watering cacti plants is by immersing them in a tub of water to make them as much water as they can so that they can go on for a while. These plants appreciate natural light.

Aloe Vera

Aloe vera, like cactus plants are succulents and belong to the leafy succulent family. They require little watering and can go on for three weeks without any watering. The top surface has to completely dry out before watering this plant. If you are not sure when you last watered the plant then simply push a knuckle into the topsoil to see how damp it is. It should be dry for at least two inches on top before you start watering it again. These plants will do well in a bright spot but try not to keep it on a windowsill. The plant's leaves can be used in many ways to find relief from a whole host of conditions including skin infections to stomach upsets.

Air Plants

Air plants are unique, as they do not have any roots. They instead use their tentacle like leaves to absorb water. It is great for those who do not have the patience to water their plants. A good way to water the plants is by immersing the whole plant into a tub of water until the pot is full. These plants are usually hung on the walls. It is best to place them in glass terrariums and will do well when mounted on wooden plaques. Spray the leaves with water or wipe it down with a damp cloth from time to time to keep the leaves dust free.

Spider Plants

Spider plants are quite popular and extremely hardy. They are preferred for their unique look. They are capable of eliminating the pollution in any space. They are great plants to have around as their leaves have the capacity to produce smaller leaves that are better known as babies. It is best to water it once a week to give the plants enough water to last the whole week. These plants love bright light and will do well under a bright bulb. Plant these in hanging planters and hang the pots from high top so that the leaves can cascade down.

Snake Plants

Snake plants are also known as Sansevieria or mother in law's tongue owing to their shape and structure. They are characterized by long thin leaves that have a pointed tip. They require very little to no care. In fact, they will do very well if you ignore them and produce long leaves that require no care. It hardly needs any watering in the winters. Water it just twice a month in the summers. Snake plants will do well in rooms that have very little light and do well in a bright spot.

Echeveria

This plant is a succulent and will do well with erratic watering. They love light and will produce lovely little blooms under bright light. They will do well on windowsills. It needs well-draining soil and water only after the topsoil has dried. These will do well in small pots. They look great on the bedroom side table as the whole plant looks like one giant flower.

Ivy

Ivy plants are great as indoor ornamental plants. They will do well on the topmost shelves as the leaves can cascade downwards and grow to your liking. They are usually placed in kitchens but will also look great in living rooms. The plants prefer light soil that is well draining. They love indirect light and will do well under bright lights.

Ways to keep houseplants, indoor plants, office plants healthy

- If you are bringing plants indoors from outdoors then make sure they are healthy and free from pests and insects. If there are any then use a natural pesticide like neem oil to get rid of them.

- Try not to place houseplants in areas that are not ideal for them such as air conditioning ducts or televisions as they can negatively impact the plant's growth.

- Add a pebble tray below the pots to absorb any excess moisture and maintain humidity levels in the pots.

- Use sterile pots as that can control the growth of fungus over the plants.

Conclusion

I want to thank you for purchasing this book. I hope it proved to be an informative and an enjoyable read.

Now that you know everything there is to know about small space gardening, I am sure that you are excited to plant your garden. Small space gardening will help save your time and make the most of the space that's available to you. There are different ideas for a small space garden discussed in this book and they are all pretty easy to implement. You can start with one or all of these ideas; it is entirely up to you. You can have a container garden in your kitchen to grow herbs, a vertical garden on an outside wall, and a hanging planter in your living room or perhaps a raised bed on your front porch. If not, you can always place a couple of pots on your balcony or on the terrace to grow a variety of plants. You can grow fruit, vegetables, herbs and different edible flowers in a small space garden. It is easy to maintain a small space garden if you follow the simple tips given in this book.

Now, all that you need to do is select an idea for your small space garden and get started.

Your feedback is very valuable. It is important to me to know your opinion and experience of this book so that I can continue to improve it and publish better books for you in the future. Please do leave an honest review on Amazon or alternatively send me an Email at andre@urbanehaus.com. I would appreciate your input. Many thanks.

If you are interested in Gardening ideas please check out my other books below.

The Indoor Herb Gardeners' Companion: From Propagation to Preservation

Greenhouse Gardening: A Victorian Fantasy - Mastering Greenhouse Principles

Find out more about us and what we do at urbanehaus.com

Made in the USA
Middletown, DE
19 February 2019